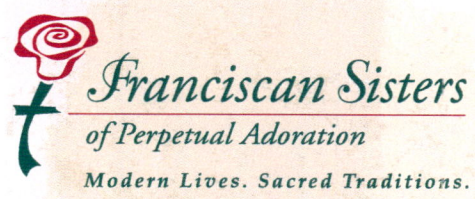

THE WAY IN THE 21st CENTURY

is a publication of the Franciscan Sisters of Perpetual Adoration.

Acknowledgement

Special thank you to Franciscan Sister of Perpetual Adoration Jean Moore
who supported and reviewed this work. While Sister Jean is no longer with us,
her message to me and to all of us is reflected inside these pages:
"Never forget who you are."

Franciscan Sisters of Perpetual Adoration

912 Market Street • La Crosse, WI 54601
(608) 782-5610 (phone) • (608) 782-6301 (fax)
email: affiliation@fspa.org
fspa.org

Table of Contents

INTRODUCTION

"The Way," derived from the Hebrew word "halakha," meaning the "way of life," is the name given to the early Jewish communities who were attracted to Jesus and his teachings. Many of these early followers never knew Jesus personally but were deeply affected by his message, understanding their faith to touch every aspect of living. In reaching out to the Gentiles (non-Jewish people) as part of their mission, communities grew and Christianity was born.

Who are the Gentiles now, or who would be considered the "other"? Why does this question matter? The number of Americans belonging to a church, mosque or synagogue is at an all-time low. In the article "In U.S., Decline of Christianity Continues at Rapid Pace," Pew Research Center reported on Oct. 17, 2019, at pewforum.org, that the percentage of U.S. adults with no religious affiliation had doubled in less than 30 years. This trend is projected to continue.

In an era of heightened social and political discourse, we are also experiencing a loss of common language in our values and identity. As people of the 21st century, we face a world with unique opportunities and challenges. It is time again to claim The Way, to reach out to those unfamiliar to us and find a common ground within our relationships, community and the Earth.

A SPIRITUAL FRAMEWORK

In "Why the only future worth building includes everyone," his TED Talk shared on April 25, 2017, at ted.com, Pope Francis says, "Life flows through our relations with others. ... none of us is an island, an autonomous and independent 'I' separated from the other, and we can only build the future by standing together, including everyone." In his encyclical, "Fratelli Tutti: On Fraternity and Social Friendship," Pope Francis further emphasizes a culture of encounter and dialogue that respects "the truth of our human dignity" and recognizes that the whole is "greater than the sum of its parts."

Often unknown to the general public, religious sisters (commonly referred to as nuns) have embraced this understanding in their communities. Faithful to the teachings of the Catholic Church, they recognize every human being to have one of three vocations: religious life, single life or married life. The Catechism of the Catholic Church emphasizes the sacredness and meaning of these vocations. "Love is the fundamental and innate vocation of every human being."

> **" Life flows through our relations with others. ... we can only build the future by standing together, including everyone. "**
>
> **~ Pope Francis**

Women and men who desire to live a more meaningful and purposeful life in their vocation can become affiliates or associates (other titles exist as well) of a religious community in which many highlight that everyone is invited, all faith traditions or none. According to "Growing number of associates partner with religious communities to quench spiritual thirst" by Dan Stockman, published on July 18, 2016, at globalsistersreport.org, there were nearly 56,000 associates in the United States and Canada affiliated with religious communities at that time. Many of these religious congregations continue to sponsor spirituality centers and provide volunteer opportunities in social justice efforts. Religious communities are hidden gems that offer a unique and welcoming spiritual home.

UNIVERSAL VALUES

Too often we are set apart from one another based on our differing beliefs and backgrounds.

Too often we box God in and draw lines that define what God is and isn't based on what's comfortable to us. Too often we are divided by labels, yet there is a collective wisdom that unites us much more than what separates us. The Golden Rule, the principle of treating others as one would wish to be treated, is found in the majority of religions and cultures throughout the world. Although God has many names and understandings, our experience of faith is quite universal, often more so than what is culturally recognized. When we sense the interconnectedness of all things and choose to live our life through a spiritual lens, we are changed from the inside out. Our values become a way of life.

Within the context of religious orders, communities were built upon shared values of their religious founders, many of which still exist in major world religions today. The Franciscan Sisters of Perpetual Adoration frame their ministry from the lives of St. Francis and St. Clare of Assisi. These founders lived with religious wars and famine during the tumultuous years of the Crusades.

Francis, a soldier and later a captive of war, learned how important it was to lead a spiritual life that included dialogue with everyone. To explore peace with his Muslim brothers and sisters, he set out to meet the Sultan of Egypt, Malik al-Kamil. This experience is detailed in Mark Pattison's article, "In 1219, St. Francis crossed Crusade lines to meet Egypt's sultan. What can we learn from their encounter?," published at americamagazine.org on Dec. 8, 2017. Instead of subjecting him to capital punishment, which was expected during wartime, al-Kamil welcomed Francis into his dwelling place.

> " **Too often we are divided by labels, yet there is a collective wisdom that unites us much more than what separates us.** "

THE GOLDEN RULE

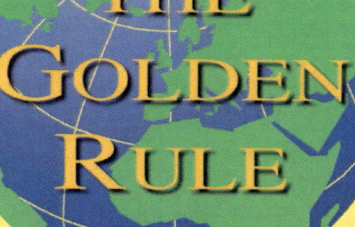

Hinduism
This is the sum of duty:
do not do to others what would
cause pain if done to you
Mahabharata 5:1517

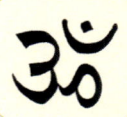

Buddhism
Treat not others in ways
that you yourself would
find hurtful
The Buddha, Udana-Varga 5.18

Bahá'í Faith
Lay not on any soul a load
that you would not wish to
be laid upon you, and
desire not for
anyone the
things you
would not
desire for
yourself
Baha'u'llah, Gleanings

Confucianism
One word which sums up the
basis of all good conduct...
loving-kindness.
Do not do to
others what
you do not
want done
to yourself
Confucius, Analects 15.23

Islam
Not one of you truly believes
until you wish for others what
you wish for yourself
The Prophet Muhammad, Hadith

Taoism
Regard your neighbour's gain
as your own gain, and your
neighbour's loss as your own loss
Lao Tzu, T'ai Shang Kan Ying P'ien, 213-218

Judaism
What is hateful to you,
do not do to your neighbour.
This is the whole Torah;
all the rest is commentary
Hillel, Talmud, Shabbat 31a

Sikhism
I am a stranger to no one;
and no one is a stranger
to me. Indeed, I am
a friend to all
Guru Granth Sahib, p. 1299

Jainism
One should treat all
creatures in the world
as one would like
to be treated
Mahavira, Sutrakritanga

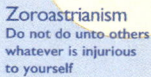

Christianity
In everything, do to others
as you would have them
do to you; for this is the
law and the prophets
Jesus, Matthew 7:12

Zoroastrianism
Do not do unto others
whatever is injurious
to yourself
Shayast-na-Shayast 13.29

**Native
Spirituality**
We are as much alive
as we keep the earth alive
Chief Dan George

Unitarianism
We affirm and promote respect
for the interdependent web of all
existence of which we are a part
Unitarian principle

For days these strangers talked about the spiritual life and found common ground, as discussed at sultanandthesaintfilm.com. It is a story of radical inclusiveness and transformation which many faith traditions and religious communities can relate to in their sacred stories. It illustrates to us the universal message of the Golden Rule.

“ It is a story of radical inclusiveness and transformation ... ”

Painting of the Sultan and St. Francis displayed in the Church of Capuchinos, Cordoba, Spain

So how do we travel this path together in today's climate? How do we move toward a shared vision that relates to our daily lived experiences? What Way can we find in common, with all our similarities and differences, to build bridges within our relationships, community and the Earth?

The following chapters are intended to answer these questions framed within the universal values of reflection, presence, simplicity, humility, peacemaking, stewardship and service. As with all commitments, a continued practice or discipline within a framework is required. Most of us could not wake up one morning and choose to run a marathon without months of prior training to condition our bodies. Likewise, understanding the paradoxical complexities of quantum physics requires study and education. We too find great difficulty leading a spiritual or intentional life without naming and committing to our values.

Chapter 1

REFLECTION

PRAYER/CONTEMPLATION

To be reflective is to examine who we are in relationship to ourselves and others. In doing so, we open ourselves to the spiritual nature of our existence. Defined broadly, this process is prayer. FSPA charism is built upon this wisdom with a rich history of perpetual adoration.

In Thomas Merton's "New Seeds of Contemplation," he described a state of reflection with open and inviting language. "It is spiritual wonder. It is spontaneous awe at the sacredness of life, of being. It is gratitude for life, for awareness and for being. It is a vivid realization of the fact that life and being in us proceed from an invisible, transcendent and infinitely abundant Source. Contemplation is, above all, awareness of the reality of that Source ... [it] goes both beyond reason and beyond simple faith. It is a more profound depth of faith, a knowledge too deep to be grasped in images, in words or even in clear concepts."

Reflection calls us to worship, to a prayerful and reverential attitude toward the Source, one another and all of creation. It recognizes that which is in motion beyond us and beyond our ego. In our fast-paced, instant gratification culture, it can be extremely difficult to give space and time for reflection.

Consider carving out solitude and silence as a routine practice in your life that provides time for prayer and contemplation. Give yourself permission to turn the radio off during your commute, go for a walk alone in nature or sit in stillness at home. Religious settings such as a church, mosque or synagogue also offer welcoming spaces to practice this.

David Foster Wallace, a famous author on the topic of American culture, stated in his 2005 "This Is Water: Some Thoughts, Delivered on a Significant Occasion, about Living a Compassionate Life" commencement speech given at Kenyon College in Gambier, Ohio, that "The most obvious, important realities are often the ones that are hardest to see and talk about. ... It means being conscious and aware enough to choose what you pay attention to and to choose how you construct meaning from experience. ... There is no such thing as not worshipping. Everybody worships. The only choice we get is what to worship.

"And the compelling reason for maybe choosing some sort of god or spiritual-type thing to worship — be it J.C. or Allah, be it Yahweh or the Wiccan mother-goddess or the Four Noble Truths or some inviolable set of ethical principles — is that pretty much anything else you worship will eat you alive. If you worship money and things — if they are where you tap real meaning in life — then you will never have enough. Never feel you have enough. It's the truth. Worship your own body and beauty and sexual allure and you will always feel ugly ... On one level we all know this ... it's been codified as myths, proverbs, clichés, epigrams, parables: the skeleton of

every great story. The whole trick is keeping the truth up front in daily consciousness."

Naturally, reflection leads us to examine our beliefs. Do we have to believe the same things in order to do this together? Our beliefs or faith can be best understood as a journey — not a destination. Anne Lamott, an American novelist and writer on spiritual matters, is well-known for defining faith as a verb and states in her book, "Plan B: Further Thoughts on Faith," that "The opposite of faith is not doubt, but certainty. Certainty is missing the point entirely." Richard Rohr, a Franciscan priest and popular author, shared a similar sentiment in "Oneing: Innocence." "The opposite of faith is not doubt; the opposite of faith is control." Welcoming our different beliefs on this path is relinquishing a false sense of security and control.

Consider who and/or what you worship. How does this show up in your life and the lives of those you love? Are you being called to let go of anything in your understanding of faith?

AWARENESS

An important step in reflection is an awareness of our environment. In this technological age, we are inundated with information and superficial connections. We are changing how we attempt to satisfy our innate human need to belong.

When we can carve out precious free time in the day, many of us occupy it by scrolling through Facebook, Twitter or other social media platforms. What we witness in return is mostly a false reality; seldom do we see the mundane aspects of daily life or the natural struggles that are a part of healthy relationships. It is actually relating to these things that give us the greatest sense of belonging.

Cell phone notifications, emails and texts also divide our attention. In "The Gifts of Imperfection: Let Go of Who You Think You're Supposed to Be and Embrace Who You Are," Brené Brown wrote candidly, "I can't tell you how many times I've walked into a restaurant and seen two parents on their cell phones while their kids are busy texting or playing video games. What's the point of even sitting together?" In an age of global connectedness, we find ourselves less connected than ever before.

Consider rethinking the time you allow technology and devices to occupy your life. What if you browsed social media only during a designated day or time of the week? What challenge can you create to limit your cell phone use? What would these boundary settings give more space to? What else in your environment keeps you from living intentionally?

SELF-LOVE

Another important aspect of reflection is self-love. From a spiritual perspective, this journey begins with examining the relationship between God and love.

Franciscan theologian John Duns Scotus suggested that Jesus came as an act of love by God, independent of human sin. This understanding of God is an essence of unconditional love with no strings attached, no conditions and no limitations. Do we relate to God in this way: understanding Divine Mystery as a relationship of love and entirely free? Another influential Franciscan theologian, St. Bonaventure, understood God as not just loving, but Love itself, as evidenced in "Discovering the Franciscan Intellectual Tradition: A Life-Giving Vision" by John V. Kruse.

Our capacity to love others directly relates to our capacity to love ourselves, which poses some important questions. Do we love ourselves unconditionally? Who am I at my core? What are my personality behaviors and patterns? What motivates me? As we come to understand and accept our strengths and limitations, we become free to move within them and beyond them. Through love we become our most real selves. Through love we find God.

How do you see the relationship between God and love? Consider asking a close loved one how they perceive your passions and frustrations. You might also journal on this topic. What can you learn by reflecting on your sense of identity? How does this connect to your understanding of God?

The Golden Rule by Norman Rockwell
Mosaic presented to the United Nations

Chapter 2

PRESENCE

GOODNESS/BEAUTY

An important value to integrate into our daily lives is to be present to the goodness and beauty in one another and in creation. In his poem, "Canticle of Brother Sun and Sister Moon," St. Francis of Assisi shared his witness to the goodness and beauty around him.

Most High, all-powerful, good Lord,
Yours are the praises, the glory, and the honor, and all blessing,
To You alone, Most High, do they belong,
And no human is worthy to mention your name.
Praised be You, my Lord, with all Your creatures,
Especially Sir Brother Sun,
Who is the day and through whom You give us light.
And he is beautiful and radiant with great splendor;
And bears a likeness of You, Most High One.
Praised be You, my Lord, through Sister Moon and the stars,
In heaven You formed them clear and precious and beautiful.
Praised be You, my Lord, through Brother Wind,
And through the air, cloudy and serene, and every kind of Weather,
Through whom You give sustenance to Your creatures.
Praised be You, my Lord, through Sister Water,
Who is very useful and humble and precious and chaste.
Praised be You, my Lord, through Brother Fire,
Through whom You light the night,
And he is beautiful and playful and robust and strong.
Praised be You, my Lord, through our Sister Mother Earth,
Who sustains and governs us,
And who produces various fruits with colored flowers and herbs.
Praised be You, my Lord, through those who give pardon for Your love,
And bear infirmity and tribulation.
Blessed are those who endure in peace,
For by You, Most High, shall they be crowned.

As revealed in this writing, St. Francis developed a deep awareness that he was related to all things, no matter how small, because everything reflected the goodness of God. For him, being present to one another in relationship was a way to mirror God's presence to us in creation. He considered this a calling and important ministry, as detailed in "Build with Living Stones" from Franciscan Institute Publications.

MINDFULNESS

Recognizing beauty and goodness brings forth a sense of wonder and awe and calls us to the present moment. This presence can also be understood as a form of mindfulness.

In "The Miracle of Mindfulness: An Introduction to the Practice of Meditation," Buddhist monk Thich Nhat Hanh states, "People usually consider walking on water or in thin air a miracle. But I think the real miracle is not to walk either on water or in thin air, but to walk on earth. Every day we are engaged in a miracle which we don't even recognize: a blue sky, white clouds, green leaves, the black, curious eyes of a child — our own two eyes. All is a miracle."

Mindfulness can be defined as the practice of maintaining a nonjudgmental state of heightened or complete awareness of one's thoughts, emotions or experiences on a moment-to-moment basis. Further details are described in "What Is Mindfulness?," an article at greatergood berkeley.edu. It can be practiced in any setting and does not involve multitasking, which is so valued in our culture.

Consider being present to the beauty and goodness around you right now. What do you see? What helps you to move into this state of mindfulness? When possible, practice the art of single-tasking. Without any other distractions, eat dinner as a family, play a board game, enjoy nature, take your spouse or friend on that much-needed date. Notice and pay attention to all the miracles around you.

LISTENING

In her youth, St. Clare of Assisi began a ministry of presence. Along with her mother and sisters, who were exiled to Perugia, she provided food to the poor and visited prisoners and the sick.

When St. Clare and her family returned to Assisi, she listened to St. Francis' preaching and was inspired to follow him. The Franciscan movement she took part in was considered radical and itinerant in nature, being open and available to go wherever necessary to serve others and share the Gospel message. She crafted the first set of monastic guidelines known to have been written by a woman and articulated a method of prayer that included gazing, considering, contemplating and imitating. As explored in "Celebrating Saint Clare of Assisi," an article at franciscanmedia.org, St. Clare believed that when we become present through prayer, we reflect God's face to the world.

An important aspect of presence is listening. Many of us can relate to the experience of sharing a joy or hardship and feeling unheard. To be in true relationship with another is to offer a listening presence. We recognize this especially when we don't receive it. In everyday conversation it is normal to respond to another's story by sharing our own. When hearing another's hardship we often attempt to help by offering a solution. Neither of

St. Clare of Assisi, stained glass image displayed in the Chapel of Notre-Dame des Flots, Sainte-Adresse, France

these responses is listening. Yet do we expect God to listen to us in this way, always giving us a sense of clear direction or an obvious answer?

Listening is a profound spiritual experience as it allows others to be present to themselves. It is an art and requires practice: often hardest to do in relationships we value the most. The following techniques, adapted from "Intentional Interviewing and Counseling: Facilitating Client Development in a Multicultural Society," a book by Allen E. Ivey, Mary Bradford Ivey and Carlos P. Zalaquett, can assist us in our presence with one another.

being PRESENT with each other

Techniques:

(1) **Attending** – Establish eye contact, sit at eye-level and pause from any task at hand; show through your behaviors that you are paying attention and care.

(2) **Exploring** – Explore as you listen. Ask, "Tell me more," or, "What is that like for you?" Resist the tendency to offer a solution or provide an answer.

(3) **Observing** – So much is said nonverbally. To show that you are present, offer observations like body language, facial expressions or tone of voice. For example, "You looked down at your hands when you said how hard this is," or, "Your eyes just lit up as you shared that."

(4) **Affirming** – What can you genuinely affirm about what you're hearing or witnessing? For example, "You've done so much already." "You care deeply about this." "You're an amazing spouse and parent," or, "Your story impacts my faith."

(5) **Paraphrasing** – Summarize key words or thoughts and allow for silence. For example, "The unknown is hard to cope with." "You have a lot on your plate and you're not sure of where to begin," or, "Life is really falling into place right now."

(6) **Reflecting Feeling** – Reflect back a feeling you've heard or a feeling the person might be experiencing. For example, "You're worried about your child." "Are you scared?" or, "You sound so excited." If the other reflects back a different feeling, that is good — the point is not really to understand a person's feelings but to invite reflection on it themselves.

(7) **Focusing** – This can be helpful when another has shared a lot of concerns or details in a story. Too often we respond based on our personal interest rather than letting the other lead. A good example might be to ask, "There is so much you shared. What concerns you most?" or, "You named so many opportunities. What's at the forefront for you?"

(8) **Reflecting Meaning** – Spirituality is directly related to our sense of meaning and purpose. Ensure that your feedback reflects this importance. For example, "This relationship is what is most important to you." "You're counting your blessings," or, "You value honesty most of all."

(9) **Normalizing** – Normalizing can be helpful with acceptance and connecting to a larger vision. Consider saying, "It's normal that you would be in shock right now." "Anyone in your shoes would be burned out. It's understandable." "Families face a lot of societal pressures. It's a real struggle," or perhaps, "Loneliness is hard to talk about."

(10) **Reframing** – Reframing invites a different way of perceiving a situation or person and can be helpful after other listening techniques are offered. For example, "You said it is really difficult to accept this and you feel stuck. Another way to think about this is now you understand more clearly who you are," or maybe, "We've spent a lot of time talking about your concerns, would it be helpful to talk about where to go from here?" Reframing is meant to be invitational, without an agenda or expectation.

Attentive listening is a sacred offering of presence. It is not meant to negate the carefreeness of casual conversations or the helpfulness of sharing concrete suggestions when asked. It is intended to be an important practice of how we care for each other in relationships. Imagine what the world could become if we all truly listened to each other.

Consider practicing these listening techniques with your loved ones. Journal about your experiences. Continue to practice them as an important value with everyone you encounter, including those who differ from you.

More and more I've come to understand that listening is one of the most important things we can do for one another. Whether the other be an adult or a child, our engagement in listening to who that person is can often be our greatest gift.

– Fred Rogers,
"Wisdom from the World According to Mister Rogers: Important Things to Remember"

Chapter 3

SIMPLICITY

Painting of St. Francis of Assisi displayed in the Church of Madonna del Sasso, Orselina, Switzerland

POVERTY

As mentioned in "St. Francis and the Foolishness of God" by Marie Dennis, Joseph Nangle and Cynthia Moe-Lobeda, St. Francis of Assisi considered the value of simplicity essential to discipleship.

Franciscan priest Murray Bodo's "Through the Year with Francis of Assisi: Daily Meditations from His Words and Life" reveals St. Francis' teachings further. "The Lord has called me into the way of simplicity and humility, and he has indeed made this way known through me and through all who choose to believe me and follow me. ... He told me I am to be a new kind of fool in this world."

Our world is full of "isms" that move us away from the value of simplicity: absolutism, dualism, consumerism, materialism, hedonism, sexism, racism, individualism, militarism and so on.

The Franciscan understanding of simplicity or poverty is to recognize our needs versus wants, alongside gratitude and reliance on God. It brings awareness of our impact on others and counteracts dishonesty and hidden agendas for one's self-interest and personal gain.

Poverty invites us into a countercultural mindset. What dominant values and behaviors in our society do you oppose? What does it look like today to be a new kind of fool?

GRATITUDE/JOY

Simplicity is often misunderstood. Do we sell half our belongings? Must we give up a vacation and donate that money to a good cause? Should we join the minimalist movement and buy a tiny house? Maybe. The answer is best found by asking this question: what is getting in the way of joyful living?

Pope Francis speaks often about spiritual happiness and joy as explained in "Pope Francis' five loves to combat the ills of today's culture," an article by Thomas Reese, published on June 6, 2018, at ncronline.org. "Consumerism only bloats the heart. It can offer occasional and passing pleasures, but not joy."

In today's culture, an important step to embrace simplicity is to examine our busyness and name how it affects our day-to-day experiences. Some of us have fallen victim to "busyism," for being busy has become a habitual practice and way of living. We often believe this is unchangeable. But is this true? Must we say "yes" to everything we are invited to? Must we commit ourselves or our family to so many activities that nearly every night is scheduled? Must we work those extra hours? What about obligations to friends? What do we actually need versus what society or others want? Is gratitude even possible in busyism?

"ENJOY THE LITTLE THINGS, FOR ONE DAY YOU MAY LOOK BACK AND REALIZE THEY WERE THE BIG THINGS." Robert Brault

Consider what you can let go of to create more simplicity in your life. Choose one thing to begin this journey. A sacred "no" can lead to a sacred "yes" along with more joyful living.

IMPACT

The Association for Living Values Education International is a collective of organizations, associations and individuals in more than 40 countries that provides professional development workshops and curriculum resources to educators. It's mission states that people around the world share basic human values and that constructive solutions to many of the challenges facing communities today will emerge more easily when there is an emphasis on a values-based approach to life.

Simplicity is among these universal values, as described at livingvalues.net:

- Simplicity is natural.
- Simplicity is learning from the Earth.
- Simplicity is beautiful.
- Simplicity is using what we already have and not wasting the Earth's material.
- Simplicity is relaxing.
- Simplicity helps create sustainable development.
- Simplicity is staying in the present and not making things complicated.
- Simplicity is enjoying a plain mind and intellect.

- Simplicity teaches us economy — how to use our resources wisely, while keeping future generations in mind.
- Simplicity is giving patience, friendship and encouragement.
- Simplicity is appreciating the small things in life.
- Simplicity is freedom from material desires and emotional desires — permission to simply "be."
- Simplicity encourages generosity and sharing.

- Simplicity is putting others first with kindness, openness and pure intentions — without expectations and conditions.

- Simplicity is learning from the wisdom of indigenous cultures.

- Simplicity calls on instinct, intuition and insight to create empathetic thoughts and feelings.

- Simplicity is appreciating inner beauty and recognizing the values of all actors, including the poor and marginalized.

- Simplicity calls upon people to rethink their values.

- Simplicity asks whether we are being induced to purchase unnecessary products. Psychological enticements create artificial needs. Desire stimulated by wanting unnecessary things results in value clashes. Greed, fear, peer pressure and a false sense of identity provide further complications. Once fulfillment of basic necessities allows for a comfortable lifestyle, extremes and excesses invite indulgence and waste.

- Simplicity helps decrease the gap between the haves and have nots, by demonstrating the logic of true economics to earn, save, invest and share the sacrifices and prosperity. As a result, all people enjoy a better quality of life, regardless of where they were born.

Simplicity also recognizes that everything is gift. When we relax, stay present and appreciate the small things in life, we more clearly see and experience this. When we understand that the Earth's resources are limited and tend to the planet's care, we come to greater appreciation of clean air and access to water. Simplicity is as much an attitude as it is an action that leads us to a greater understanding of ourselves and our place in the universe.

When has simplicity led to more clarity in your life? How did it have an impact on others? What aspects of simplicity as listed stand out and call your attention? Plan your first step to get there.

"Hope" window
Mary of the Angels Chapel
St. Rose Convent
La Crosse, Wisconsin

Chapter 4

HUMILITY

ACCEPTANCE

To embrace humility is to recognize our true self before God and to see God in everything and everyone.

Max Warren, a Christian missionary, wrote about this eloquently as shared in "Why we should dare to visit the holy ground of other cultures," an article published on Oct. 18, 2017, at christiantoday.com. "Our first task in approaching another people, another culture, another religion, is to take off our shoes, for the place we are approaching is holy. Else we may find ourselves treading on [people's] dreams. More serious still, we may forget that God was here before our arrival."

The journey of humility begins with self. As we accept our strengths and limitations, we find an inner freedom from having to protect our hidden self from others. This self-acceptance gives us the ability to accept others as they are. A place of humility also enables us to genuinely see and hear those around us providing space for

all of our vulnerabilities. How often do we avoid relationships because of fear of intimacy or rejection, or because we harmed a person and are unable to face it? What about those we don't like, or those who are different from us religiously, politically, sexually, culturally and so on? To value humility is to challenge ourselves to move beyond these barriers.

Relationships are complex. Entire fields of study focus solely on this concept. Some of our relationships warrant more attention than others, like those with our partner, children, extended family, blended family or friends. In our individualistic society with a strong orientation toward autonomy, we run the risk of assuming that focus on relationships of no benefit to us is a sign of weakness.

And when little to no cultural value is emphasized in reaching out to those different from us, we can be left with misconceptions about who the "other" is. Are we seeing this dynamic and lack of humility in our society today?

Consider a relationship that needs repair and reflect on humility in your reactions. What have you learned? How has your autonomy served you positively? Negatively?

MINORES/PRIVILEGE

There is an important relationship between our attitude of humility (also known as "minores" in the Franciscan tradition) and privilege.

The origin of the term privilege in the United States dates back to the 1910 publication "Social Equities" from the National Council of the Congregational Churches of the United States. "What infinite cruelties and injustices have been practiced by men who believed that to have a white skin constituted special privilege and who reckoned along with the divine rights of kings the divine rights of the white!"

Privilege can be defined as a set of unearned benefits given to people who fit into a specific social group, due to aspects of their identity such as male, white, English-speaking, middle class, heterosexual and Christian. These benefits are due to constructs of a social system. This is a key understanding, as privilege is often misunderstood and regarded individually rather than systemically.

Barack Obama was often referred to as a "Black president" by the media while previous white presidents were referred to simply as "president." Dissimilar treatment due to a person's non-white race is an example of white privilege.

In the case of most religions, God is predominantly referred to in the masculine sense, such as "Father," or with the pronoun "He." While recognizing this, the Catechism of the Catholic Church states clearly, "God is the first origin of everything ... is goodness and loving ... transcends the human distinction between the sexes. ... is neither man nor woman ... transcends human fatherhood and motherhood." To be accustomed to predominantly masculine language for a genderless God is male privilege.

As a 14-year-old student at The Paideia School in Atlanta, Georgia, Royce Mann was filmed reciting his poem, "White Boy Privilege." The video, posted on YouTube on June 27, 2016, includes this excerpt.

Dear women, I'm sorry. Dear Black people, I'm sorry.
Dear Asian Americans, dear Native Americans,
Dear immigrants who come here seeking a better life, I'm sorry.
Dear everyone who isn't a middle or upper-class white boy, I'm sorry.
I have started life on the top of the ladder while you were born on the first rung.
To be honest I'm scared of what it would be like if I wasn't on the top rung,
If the tables were turned,
And I didn't have my white boy privilege safety blankie to protect me.
If I lived a life lit by what I lack, not what I have,
If I lived a life in which when I failed, the world would say, "Told you so."
If I lived the life that you live.
When I was born I had a success story already written for me.
You — you were given a pen and no paper.
I've always felt that that's unfair,
But I've never dared to speak up because I've been too scared.
Well now I realize that there's enough blankie to be shared.
Everyone should have the privileges I have.
In fact they should be rights instead.
Everyone's story should be written, so all they have to do is get it read.
Enough said. No, not enough said.
It is embarrassing that we still live in a world,
In which we judge another person's character,
By the size of their paycheck,
The color of their skin,
Or the type of chromosomes they have.
I know it wasn't us eighth-grade white boys who created this system,
But we profit from it every day.
We don't notice these privileges though,
Because they don't come in the form of things we gain,
But rather the lack of injustices that we endure.
I get that change can be scary, but equality shouldn't be.
It's time to let go of that fear.
It's time to take that ladder and turn it into a bridge.

Consider privilege within the context of culture and religion. Picture Jesus for a moment. Does he have olive-brown skin, dark eyes and black hair? What image do you have for God? How has privilege impacted your faith?

HOSPITALITY

From a place of humility, we can provide genuine hospitality and respect for one another.

In his article, "Religious Hospitality: A Spiritual Practice for Congregations," published at uuabookstore.org, Peter Morales, the first Latino president of the Unitarian Universalist Association, describes this as a critical spiritual practice for congregations:

- Hospitality, true hospitality, is emotionally powerful. It touches something very deep in us — our profound human longing to feel accepted, to belong, to be loved, to feel safe, to be valued and respected. ... A congregation in which people do not genuinely love each other is not likely to exude warmth. A congregation that is self-absorbed and disconnected from its community cannot offer religious hospitality. Hospitality is love in action.

- The world's great religious traditions have long affirmed the link between religion and hospitality. Both Hebrew and Christian scriptures admonish us to welcome the stranger as a guest. Hebrew scriptures, recalling the oppression the children of Israel suffered as foreigners, teach us to love the stranger, the outsider. The Book of Leviticus instructs people to "love the alien as yourself, for you were aliens in the land of Egypt."

- The teachings of Jesus extend this tradition. Jesus and his followers went beyond welcoming the foreigner to the more radical practice of welcoming the marginalized: children, women, tax collectors, the poor, lepers, prostitutes, even enemies. In Jesus' vision of the Kingdom of God there are no foreigners. We are all God's children and we are all loved.

- The Buddhist tradition arrives at a similar place by a different road. In some ways the Buddhist perspective is the most radical. Buddhism teaches that the very distinction between one group and another, between insider and outsider, between citizen and alien, is a dangerous illusion.

- A true religious hospitality reaches out to those we do not yet know. ... The hunger for true religious community, for connection and commitment, is pervasive in our time. Our future depends on whether we can connect with people at the level of their deepest longings and highest aspirations. We are called to feed the spiritually hungry and to offer a home to the religiously homeless. And in the process, we are enriched in spirit.

Hospitality goes beyond welcoming those we do not yet know. It is also being open to the diversity of thoughts, behaviors and values of another, especially of those aspects that cause us to rethink our own. The United States Conference of Catholic Bishops created a resource for parishes in welcoming immigrants and asylum seekers into their communities while fostering a greater understanding of diversity among its members. Aligning with Catholic social teaching, "Welcoming the Stranger Parish Guide: Unity in Diversity" is available at usccb.org.

Consider the practice of hospitality. Is there a neighbor, coworker, family member, friend or stranger who could benefit from a welcoming gesture or a random act of kindness? What differences in thoughts, behaviors or values have caused you to rethink your own? What changed in you as a result?

Chapter 5

PEACEMAKING

St. Francis of Assisi, stained glass image displayed in the Church of St. James the Greater, Porto Azzurro, Elba, Italy

CONVERSION

St. Francis centered his ministry on peace, as written in "Legend of the Three Companions" by Brothers Leo, Angelo and Rufino.

"Since you speak of peace, all the more so must you have it in your hearts. Let none be provoked to anger or scandal by you, but rather may they be drawn to peace and good will, to [kindness] and [harmony] through your gentleness. We have been called to heal wounds, to unite what has fallen apart and to bring home those who have lost their way."

"The Prayer of St. Francis," first found in 1912 in a spiritual magazine, The Little Bell, was submitted without an author (although some speculate that Catholic priest Esther Bouquerel, the editor of the publication, wrote it). It was heavily publicized during World War I and World War II. Most of us, due to the universality of its message of peace, are familiar with it today.

Lord, make me an instrument of your peace.
Where there is hatred let me sow love;
Where there is injury, pardon;
Where there is doubt, faith;
Where there is despair, hope;
Where there is darkness, light;
Where there is sadness, joy.
O Divine Master, grant that I may not so much seek
To be consoled as to console;
To be understood as to understand;
To be loved as to love.
For it is in giving that we receive;
It is in pardoning that we are pardoned;
And it is in dying that we are born to eternal life.

This Franciscan prayer outlines the value of ongoing conversion — the act of continually opening oneself up for growth and change, and invites us to confront ourselves honestly. Where do we need this most? Where is peace most often broken? Generally, in our intimate relationships we are operating as our most authentic selves. Taking an honest look into how we are in our relationships is one pathway to conversion. Surprisingly at times, this openness to transformation can bring about an amazing sense of peace within.

RELATIONSHIPS/TRANSFORMATION

The field of psychology is devoted to repairing and deepening our sense of self, including within relationships.

Anthropologist and pastor Gary Chapman developed a theory on personality preferences for giving and receiving love, "The 5 Love Languages: The Secret to Love That Lasts." He wrote that we all experience love differently and to understand our love languages is to understand the communication barriers we often miss. In short, the five languages can be described as,

1. **Words of Affirmation –** This language uses words to affirm other people.

2. **Acts of Service –** For these people, actions speak louder than words.

3. **Receiving Gifts –** For some people, what makes them feel most loved is to receive a gift.

4. **Quality Time –** This language is all about giving the other person your attention.

5. **Physical Touch –** To these people, nothing speaks more deeply than appropriate touch.

Are we aware of how we show our love to those closest to us? Have we made judgments in our relationships that we might reconsider? How can we become more honest as parents or caregivers of children?

Licensed marriage and family therapist Hal Runkel has focused his career on family dynamics and writes about it in his blog, Peace Begins with Pause, at screamfree.com. In his book, "ScreamFree Parenting: The Revolutionary Approach to Raising Your Kids by Keeping Your Cool," he outlines how we scream (including yelling, disconnecting ourselves, overcompensating, threatening, withholding love and labeling) and suggests how to instead create peace, stop emotional reactivity and stay connected. According to the ScreamFree movement, "When you respond more, and react less, you can learn to handle any moment, in the moment."

In the "Prayer of St. Francis," consoling, understanding and loving one another is emphasized. When we focus on this attending in our relationships, we receive much more than we give: our openness to diversity grows, our compassion deepens and we reflect more peace in our presence. Similarly, in the process of self-forgetting and pardoning we let go of fear and allow our vulnerabilities to strengthen our relationships. To take seriously our vocation or calling is to become an instrument of peace.

Consider opportunities to confront yourself honestly within your relationships. How can the teachings of the "Prayer of St. Francis" and psychology support your ability for peacemaking?

FORGIVENESS

Peacemaking is impossible without forgiveness.

In his book, "No Future Without Forgiveness," South African Anglican priest and human rights activist Desmond Tutu discusses the path to peace: "Forgiving and being reconciled are not about pretending that things are other than they are. It is not patting one another on the back and turning a blind eye to the wrong. True reconciliation exposes the awfulness, the abuse, the pain, the degradation, the truth." In Christianity and most religions, forgiveness is held in high value. Forgiveness invites us to ongoing conversion, to separate the person from the behavior and to recognize limitations of others and ourselves. It is a process of continued integration and often has to be revisited due to reminders or situations that can reopen our wounds. Keeping in mind the importance of physical and emotional safety, including setting healthy boundaries, relationships call for our forgiveness. When centered on true reconciliation, we leave ourselves open to being transformed. Suffering not transformed is transmitted. Forgiveness and pardoning give us the freedom to be at peace.

If you are experiencing a difficult relationship right now, name what needs forgiveness in order to begin your journey of healing. Is there anything you might need to forgive within yourself? Do you need to forgive a loved one who has passed? Do you need to forgive God?

Chapter 6

STEWARDSHIP

ECOLOGY/JUSTICE

Stewardship can be defined as our responsibility to care for the Earth's resources and the needs of the poor and marginalized.

Pope Francis' encyclical on the environment and human ecology, "Laudato Si': On Care for Our Common Home," emphasizes this critical moment in the Earth's history and urgently calls the world to respond. Eco-justice values ecology and justice together, understanding that there is little environmental health without socioeconomic justice, and vice versa. This is further discussed in "What is Eco-Justice?," an article published April 26, 2017, at spsmw.org by the Sisters of Providence. When fully understanding the environmental crisis we face, we can feel paralyzed. How can we make an impact? Where do we find hope?

To truly embrace the value of stewardship, especially in today's culture, the relationship between religion and science must be addressed. There appears to be an increasing schism between the two fields rooted primarily in a lack of understanding. An important step in finding hope is to recognize this truth and break down the barriers.

Conflict arises for some from the very beginning in the understanding of creation. The Catechism of the Catholic Church provides this statement for interpretation of Scripture: "In order to discover the sacred authors' intention, the reader must take into account the conditions of their time and culture, the literary genres in use at that time, and the modes of feeling, speaking and narrating ... For the fact is that truth is differently presented and expressed in the various types of historical writing, in prophetical and poetical texts, and in other forms of literary expression."

Literary genres that exist in biblical text include prose, poetry, myth, law codes, historical narrative, parable, allegory, legend, saga and more. The two creation stories found in the Book of Genesis fit into the literary genre of myth; a use of imaginary symbols and images that speak to a spiritual message of God and creation — not to be misunderstood as stories of historical or scientific facts. The creation myths and other literary expressions found within Scripture are well explained by Catholic biblical scholar Margaret Nutting Ralph in her book, "And God Said What?: An Introduction to Biblical Literary Forms." Dianne Bergant, a member of the Congregation of Sisters of St. Agnes, also shares incredible insight into literary forms expressed in the Bible in her book, "Scripture: History and Interpretation."

According to their mission, the Vatican Observatory, located just outside of Rome, Italy, was established to show that "the Church and her Pastors are not opposed to true and solid science, whether human or divine, but that they embrace it, encourage it, and promote it with the fullest possible dedication." Their mission states further at vaticanobservatory.va,

"Where in the 19th century, the Church felt t had to tell scientists that they shouldn't be afraid of religion; now, our mission is to remind churchgoers that there's nothing to be afraid of in science. ... We are like a bridge ... between the world of science and the world of faith, to give testimony that it is possible to believe in God and to be good scientists." Just as the understanding of creation is debated, so too is the reality of our climate crisis. In Laudato Si', Pope Francis not only embraces the scientific findings of climate change; he names the environmental crisis as a moral and religious matter as well.

Underestimating the connection between culture and religion can lead to defensiveness when facing different viewpoints or new learnings. Is your familiarity to religion related to your exposure as a child? What different/new religious experiences have you explored as an adult? How do you understand the relationship between religion and science?

SUSTAINABILITY

The United Nations created Sustainable Development Goals as a blueprint to achieve a better and more sustainable future for all. Global challenges we face, including those related to poverty, inequality, climate, environmental degradation, prosperity, and peace and justice are addressed.

The following suggestions are offered within these goals for individuals:

- Donate what you don't use: 700 million people live in extreme poverty.
- Waste less food and support local farmers.
- Vaccinate your family to protect them and improve public health.
- Help educate the children in your community.
- Empower women and girls and ensure their equal rights: 1 in 3 women has experienced physical and/or sexual violence.
- Avoid wasting water. Water scarcity affects more than 40% of the world's population.

- Use only energy-efficient appliances and light bulbs.
- Create job opportunities for youth.
- Fund projects that provide basic infrastructure: roads, water, sanitation and electricity remain scarce in many developing countries.
- Support the marginalized and disadvantaged. Raise your voice against discrimination.
- Bike, walk or use public transportation to keep our air clean.
- Recycle paper, plastic, glass and aluminum.
- Act now to stop global warming. Global emissions of carbon dioxide (CO2) have increased by almost 50% since 1990.
- Avoid plastic bags to keep the oceans clean.
- Plant a tree and help protect the environment.
- Stand up for human rights. In 2018, the number of people fleeing war, persecution and conflict exceeded 70 million.
- Lobby your government to boost development financing.

The mission of the United Nations Sustainable Development Goals is to create dignity, peace and prosperity for all people and the planet, now and in the future. The UN recognizes that ending poverty must go hand-in-hand with strategies that build economic growth and address a range of social needs, including education, health, social protection and job opportunities, while tackling climate change and environmental protection. This is an amazing global movement we can connect to by downloading the SDGs in Action app and reviewing their resources online at un.org, including "170 Actions to Transform Our World." As the article states, "If you care about the future, be the change. Help to end poverty, to reduce inequalities and to tackle climate change. Together we can transform the world."

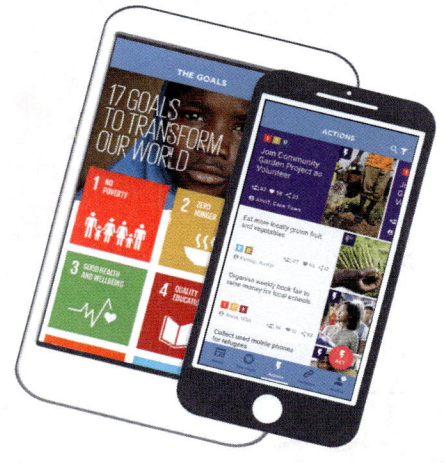

GREEN EFFORTS

Further suggestions adapted from the United States Environmental Protection Agency, taken from epa.gov, include:

- Use a tool like Household Carbon Footprint Calculator to estimate your footprint in the areas of home energy, transportation and waste.

- Learn to compost at home. Use food scraps, yard trimmings and other organic wastes to create a compost pile.

- Raise the cutting height of your lawnmower during hot summer months to keep grass roots shaded and cooler, reducing weed growth, browning and the need for watering. When you mow, "grasscycle" by leaving grass clippings on your lawn instead of bagging them. The clippings will return nutrients to the soil instead of taking up space in landfills.

- Turn off or unplug lights during the day. Doing so will save energy and help your lightbulbs last longer.

- Prevent waste by using rechargeable batteries. If you do use disposable batteries, reduce hazardous waste by buying those with low mercury content.

- For cleaning chores, buy reusable mops, rags and sponges.

- Carry food in reusable plastic or cloth bags, and drink hot and cold beverages in a thermos instead of disposable bottles or cups.

- When buying lunch, take only what you need. Too often, extra ketchup packets and napkins go to waste. Say "no" to straws.

- Eat less meat, poultry and fish. More resources are used to provide meat than those required to grow plants.

- Adjust your thermostat: lower in winter, higher in summer.

- Wash fruits and vegetables in a pan of water, not under a running faucet.

- Turn off the faucet while brushing your teeth.

- To save the paper and fossil fuels required to mail, pay your bills via e-billing programs.

- Instead of printing hard copies of your documents, save them to your hard drive or send them in an email message. Also change your printer settings to print double-sided pages.

- Reuse envelopes with metal clasps, and reuse file folders by covering old labels with new ones.

- Purchase recycled paper and keep a recycling bin near your desk.

- Buy energy efficient items with the ENERGY STAR® logo.

- Before replacing a computer that no longer fits your needs, consider enhancing the computer's capacity by upgrading the hard drive or memory. This can save you money, too.

- Donating used (but operational) electronics for reuse extends the lives of valuable products and keeps them out of the waste stream for a longer period of time. Learn where to donate your TVs, computers and other electronics by contacting your city or town hall.

- Show your commitment to a clean environment by volunteering for a cleanup effort in your community. Pick up litter anytime you see it.

- Make sure your car has a clean air filter — a dirty air filter can increase your vehicle's fuel consumption by as much as 10%.

- Think green before you shop. Bring reusable cloth bags for carrying your purchases, and try to buy items with minimal packaging and/or made with recycled content.

- Wrap gifts in recycled or reused wrapping paper.

- When gifting flowers, consider buying long-lasting silk flowers, potted plants, live bushes, shrubs or trees.

- If you host a party, set the table with cloth napkins and reusable dishes, glasses and silverware. Save and reuse party hats, decorations and favors. Be sure your guests know where to properly dispose of and recycle waste.

- Fill your dishwasher or laundry machine completely before running it. You will run fewer cycles, which saves energy and water. Also air dry when possible.

Recycling Tips

TOP 10 in the BIN

1. Cardboard
2. Paper
3. Food Boxes
4. Mail
5. Beverage Cans
6. Food Cans
7. Glass Bottles
8. Jars (plastic & glass)
9. Jugs (plastic & glass)
10. Plastic Bottles (& caps)

Do Not bag recyclables

place items loose In Cart

Recycle Wires
- Christmas lights
- extension cords
- power cords

Never Recycle
- plastic grocery bags
- batteries
- styrofoam

empty + rinse clean

Note: labels affixed to plastic, metal or glass **DO NOT** have to be removed. The recycling process takes care of this with heat.

ACTION PLAN

Consider an action plan, as illustrated in the grid below, to create more sustainable practices in your daily life. Invite others to join you in setting goals and share the journey you took to accomplish them.

GOALS/EFFORTS SUGGESTED BY THE UN AND EPA THAT I ...	What do I need in order to maintain, nurture or begin this sustainable practice?
Already Practice:	
Sometimes or Often Practice:	
Rarely or Never Practice:	

TOGETHER, WE CAN
MAKE A DIFFERENCE

SMALL CHANGES IN BEHAVIOR CAN HAVE A **BIG IMPACT** ON OUR PLANET!

WHEN YOU *THROW* SOMETHING AWAY, **WHERE DOES IT GO?**

IN THE **UNITED STATES** IN 2018,

292.4 MILLION TONS OF TRASH

WERE **GENERATED**

146.2 MILLION TONS

ENDED UP IN **LANDFILLS**

THINK GREEN BEFORE YOU SHOP

DO I NEED?
WILL I USE?
DO I ALREADY OWN?
CAN I BORROW?

HOW "GREEN" IS IT?
Companies can design their products to have as little environmental impact as possible. Do some research before buying.

REDUCE, REUSE AND RECYCLE
Rethink the materials you purchase, use and throw away.

Chapter 7

SERVICE

INTERCONNECTEDNESS

Through service, we offer our gifts and talents for the benefit of the common good.

Deciding how to begin supporting an effort or cause can be intimidating, and considering the time and attention it might take from an already busy schedule can be overwhelming. Service often requires a leap of faith as well as creativity. Could we invite a family member or friend to join us so that we can use our time for both bonding and serving others? What fits our personality best: committee involvement or something more behind-the-scenes? What causes are we especially drawn to: care of the Earth, the homeless, the trafficked, children or the elderly? Opportunities to extend a helping hand exist in our congregations, work settings, neighborhoods, schools, hospitals, community programs and more. By reaching out, we more fully understand who we are and our interconnectedness in the world.

Consider a cause you are drawn to. How will you, or do you, balance this commitment with self-care? How have you grown, or how do you hope to grow, from the experience?

MISSION/MINISTRY

The FSPA mission statement declares, "We are a community of vowed Franciscan women centered in Eucharist, committed to be loving presence through prayer, witness and service."

The FSPA affiliation mission statement affirms, "We, affiliates of the Franciscan Sisters of Perpetual Adoration, are spiritual collaborators joined in sacred relationship, supporting one another to live the Gospel and transform our world." To live the Gospel speaks to imitating the values reflected through the teachings of Jesus. From the Franciscan perspective, the values of contemplation, poverty, minores and conversion are rooted in the lives and writings of St. Francis and St. Clare as they sought to live the Gospel themselves. All lived values are to be understood as interconnected — legs of the same chair or spokes of the same wheel. Only together do they create stability and balance, and all affect one another.

St. Francis and St. Clare
Created in memory of Genevieve Gehling (mother of Franciscan Sister of Perpetual Adoration Joann Gehling) by Franciscan Sister of Perpetual Adoration Karen Kappell

COMMUNITY

Those associated with a religious congregation most often focus on three areas of commitment: prayer, ministry and community.

A time to receive, a time to give and a time to gather are understood as essential components of the spiritual life. A community offers a place of belonging, support, relationships, structure, rituals, celebrations and shared values and mission. We have come to know influential spiritual movements of the past less through spiritual teachers themselves and more through a community who believed in sharing the message and transforming the world.

Consider involvement in a community that shares your values. What is their mission? How would you know if they are a good fit? What aspects of community resonate with you, and which aspects do not?

Trust that all efforts made toward living the values of reflection, presence, simplicity, humility, peacemaking, stewardship and service significantly impact our relationships, community and the Earth. A values-based approach to life leads to a fuller existence, a life of greater meaning and purpose and a better world.

As a community may we commit to these values and invite others on the journey as well.

Together, may we find The Way.

RECEIVE

GIVE

GATHER

Sanctuary window
Design inspired by Sister Karen Kappell
St. Elizabeth Ann Seton Parish
Holmen, Wisconsin

On the cover:

The "Glory Window," designed by Gabriel Loire, is found inside the spiral-shaped chapel in Thanks-Giving Square in Dallas, Texas. The chapel affirms the reality of gratitude as a common root of religions, cultures and traditions worldwide.

Thanksgiving, which is gratitude in action, is recognized as a universal human experience. The Thanks-Giving Foundation was established to create a public space dedicated in gratitude to God and to this most ancient and enduring tradition.

Thanks-Giving Square continues to serve as common ground where people of all cultures and religions are welcome. What began as a simple park has become a refuge and space to celebrate values, thoughts and spirituality.

Franciscan Sisters
of Perpetual Adoration

Modern Lives. Sacred Traditions.

For more information on this publication, please contact
Franciscan Sisters of Perpetual Adoration
912 Market Street • La Crosse, WI 54601
(608) 782-5610 (phone) • (608) 782-6301 (fax)
email: affiliation@fspa.org
fspa.org